Online Startups

Contains 2 Manuscripts –

(How to Work from Home

And Make Money Blogging)

And (How to Start a Business and

Make Money as an Online Coach)

T. Whitmore

Table of Contents

Introduction

What is Blogging?

Picking a Niche

Choosing a Proper Platform

Focusing Fully on Content

Meeting and Socializing with other Bloggers

Write for other Bloggers

Analyzing Data

Monetizing Your Site

Maintaining Your Blog

SEO

Hone Your Creativity

Strategize Your Marketing Efforts

Rinse and Repeat

Staying in the Know

Keep Your Head above Water

Never Give up Blogging

Book 2-How to Start a Business and Make Money as an Online Coach

Introduction:

Our internet growth over the last couple of decades has caused an almighty expansion! An expansion of unlimited opportunities for individuals and private organizations all around to make lots and lots of money all over the entire globe! The world is full of myriads of competition every corner that you turn, especially online. And especially in the blogging world. When we begin to look inside of ourselves, and we mentally and intelligently think outside of the box, we can then think of alternative ways that we can make extra money. We should not concentrate on the traditional way of making money, as traditional ways take too long. Traditional ways, cut individuals off with a salary that remains somewhat stagnant and only increases minimally over the years. In this book,

Making Money From Blogging, we will be looking and thinking outside of the box, because this strategy enables individuals great successes and begins to open doors that lead into unlimited opportunities, rather than the traditional way of making money; the old nine to five.

Thinking outside of the box when it comes to making money is the only way an individual can exit a stagnant salary and leave the rat race. Billionaires and millionaires all around the globe have stated that they have taken many risks, to lead them to their fortunes. As a blogger, a career blogger, we need to be able to determine good risks and bad risks. Every business owner should definitely analyze this strategy. Also, make sure that you have a safety net of income in your bank account before you begin your blogging career full-time. Otherwise you may be eating ramen day in and day out, for pennies on the dollar. If you have a family to tend to, do not start a blogger career with zero income!

Make wise decisions, each business entrepreneur needs not only a safety net, but needs start-up costs; so before you dart at your competition, make sure that you set-up the logistics with your finances before you begin. Usually six months' worth of income is ideal, just in case you need to buy yourself time on your monthly bills. As a blogger, you don't need to be an artist who suffers financially, if you prepare yourself the right way, you can succeed with reasonable effort. But let us warn you now; succeeding in blogging requires strategically planning your finances like a game of   before you begin. Later, the money will follow you, all while you provide blogging content from the bottom of your heart. People love blogs that pour out their souls. Not in an annoying way, but an artistic type of way. If you love a topic, that's how you will come across through your online writing diction. Communication is everything in the world of blogging, learn communication strategies, and delve into the world of independent blogging.

Yes, every one of us likes money, not because we want to like it, but because we have to like it. Money moves our entire globe on a daily basis. The world works with: services, commodities, and exchanges. Of course we'd better love money, if we don't want to end up poor and on the streets and without any food. But keep in mind, this isn't always the case, as everyone needs to know that money does not create eternal happiness. We should know that relationships and experiences are really what create an ultimate meaning and belonging to human lives all around. So if your immediate goal when you start blogging is a lot of money, get out of here! Every human wants to feel accepted and wants to feel some sort of unity. Blogging can give us a sense of belonging and unity, blogging can help others as well. Blogging can help us vent. Inside of this book, *Making Money from Blogging,* you will discover chock-full information about the steps anyone can take, if you want to get serious about making money and blogging.

Yes, people blog for a full-time job now, twenty years ago, a grandmother complained about how her granddaughter was wasting her life away on her computer; twenty years later, the granddaughter is a multi-millionaire, being that she created an online app. Our guess is, the grandmother is shocked with her granddaughter's computer successes. The internet helps us individuals become limitless with the work we can produce. Are you a content genius and do you want to start seeing green dough roll inside of your bank account? Open this book if you are willing to take a moment, learn, and implement, the helpful blogging strategies inside, will be worth the knowledge. This book, *Making Money from Blogging,* was sent to you by chance, go ahead and enhance your lives and delve into this book. Watch what will unfold, we're already sold on our advice strategies.

Inside, Learn Various Blogging Method's to Make Real Money!

- Don't only learn the basics about blogging, learn the in's-and-the-out's
- Learn to provide help for each and every one of your visitors
- Provide quality blog posts, otherwise, risk your audience.
- Learn to construct a clean and sophisticated stylistic blog, and learn how to market, analyze, and monetize your blog appropriately
- Learn about yourself and your internal wants and desires
- Learn about what you don't want
- Utilize the strategies inside so that way you can provide you and your family with long-term

financial freedom. Every hard working family deserves freedom, and every blogger is grateful for their own freedom to create

- Make life better, all around, blog
- Communicate

Open this book, *Making Money from Blogging,* if you are serious about learning blogging strategies and techniques, and if you are serious about making real hard cash from your niche loving passion. Heed this advice, this is no easy task, it takes, gaining a groove and momentum, through practice, trial, and error. By learning more information, we are automatically enabling ourselves for greater things in life as bloggers. Think about it, if you learn to blog well enough, you might be able to situate your life, so you can solely work from the comfort of your own home, hence avoiding all of the world catastrophes that exist in the year 2016.

We want to help you, the blogger, get to a point where you can sit in the comfort of your pajamas, if you so choose to and work. This doesn't mean that you can be lazy at your own home; otherwise absolutely no money will be flying into your bank account. Set-up a proper office environment, this is an absolute must. Make sure your office is comfortable to work in, safe, and free of external distractions. After all, you want to get serious about starting your own blog, so let's get serious and let's start to think about your blogging career as a business, because once this business starts bringing in any kind of income, then it is darn right Uncle Sam will want a piece of your financial gains.

Yes, good old taxes! A nice office set-up, a fast internet connection, a phone, skills, willingness to learn, drive, writing and editing skills, an eye for design, and a fast working computer are all necessary components in order to get started blogging. If you have no idea about the previous components necessary to start a blog, then before you enter, brush up on your skills, as design, computer, and content skills are a must, these skills are relevant to starting a new blog. If you can't afford University training or a seminar or workshop at the moment, then the internet is a good start, as it provides a plethora of information regarding design, technical computer skills, sales, and writing advice. Brush up on each individual skill, if you need to. Continue to read if you want to learn how to start *Making Money from Blogging*. Nope, it is not a walk in the park, blogging is hard thought, so get ready to work, but in this case, you will be working and building for yourself, not a corporation. Remember, what you bring in, is all up to you.

What is Blogging?

Blogging is a new edge way to express oneself through multimedia. Blogging used to be more for content only, but as the years have advanced, and computers became more intelligent, creators all around continued to excel with their ideas. Blog's have become a conglomeration of text, photos, videos, etc. All of these forms of art can be mixed together to create a new type of media, coining the term new media arts. Blogging is a place where we can explore ourselves, our minds, and our deepest desires. Through writing and ultimate creation, we are able to experience and feel. We are also able to alleviate any stress that we may be having when we create. If you are looking to make money off of your blog, you'd better choose a topic that doesn't bore you, otherwise it is possible that you will write and post drab content, which will affect your blog in the long-run. No one wants that. You need to choose a topic that uplifts you! A topic you are incredibly excited about so your love shines through computer screens all around!

How Has Blogging Advanced?

Blogging in today's day and age has advanced because individuals all over the globe, now have access to the internet, providing a platform where individuals can explore their skills, create a killer blog, and succeed their way to their own bank account compilation. It sure is possible to succeed from blogging alone. The only blogger's who make real money have a bit of genius and hustle inside of them. Blogging has been able to unite a globe; it has also been known to spread propaganda and ill intent. Use blogging wisely in the year 2016. The access is there, formal education is not a necessity, but sure it helps. Blogging has advanced because in the year 2016 blogging has become sort of a trend, we see blogs constantly come and go on a consistent basis. This then leads us to question ourselves and our own blogs; we can start to ask ourselves certain questions like, "How can I make my blog stand out from the myriads of blogs that are currently online?" Questions like this before you begin are absolute imperative to your blogging business. If you don't ask yourself these direct questions, than it is highly possible your strategy will be all over the place, causing you to lack in quality via your precious money-maker, your blog.

Blogging Timeline

Of course curiosity is the best intent an individual can have in life, especially when it comes to learning about new skills and new ways to earn more income for your family and for yourself. Blogging started when the advent of the internet hit in the early nineties, a man by the name of Tim Berners-Lee coined the term, 'world wide web,' according to Wikipedia. We are now in the year 2016 and the birth of the internet is still fresh, it's still vibrant as ever! Blogging has never been so useful. People read all of the time and if they are reading and buying your blog services, products, memorabilia, whatever it is that you sell, well then you have tapped a market and you 'd better keep tapping, before someone else taps before you. Keep in mind, the more creative you are, the more income you will turn in. Smartphones, everyone has one in the year 2016! Even the ten year old kid down the street, they have a smartphone too! Plus ipads, iwatches, these technological gadgets are huge! This is such a huge market, so perhaps you are a writer for children's online ebooks? Well, as long as your illustrations look rad, and your content is cool, chances are the kid will want your book! Add your eBooks on your blog posts and on your blog site homepage don't forget to customize your categories and tags, as this will make it more helpful for online seekers to find you through a keyword search on Google. Sooner or later, parents will be knocking at your online blogging website looking to buy your cool and entertaining content. Use your skills! Don't ever forget how important it is to have a sense of visualization style. Remember, if your blogging page looks choppy, unedited, and the photos are grainy, yet unattractive, or unacceptable, you will lose an audience as quick as you posted all of that junk! So we wise, and hold class and professional poise!

What Determines A Successful Blog?

Since this particular book is about, '*How to Make Money Blogging,*' we can plan to measures successes by analytics and revenue brought in. Having a successful blog takes time; it can take several years, if you are not already a full-time blogger. Some blogs hit big right away, while other blogs diminish into the vast black space of the internet deep depths, never receiving any visitors. You never want to fall into a box where you don't receive any visitors. The whole point of a blog is to share content and gain the respect and the trust of your readers. Having a successful blog means that your mind and your soul are in unison, because you are actually creating and presenting topics and subjects about things you love. A successful blogs rakes in a lot of visitors, fulfills your soul, relieves your stress, honors your creativity, and brings in income.

Picking a Niche

Picking a niche is a hard task to do, especially if you have no idea what you are interested in, if you are in this boat, than soul searching to find out what you are interested in, is your best bet. In order to help you choose the niche that you want to blog about, you need to think about something that you love. Do you love to hike and explore the world? If this is so, than you might think about creating a travel blog. Are you a seasoned karate instructor? There is a lot more than you can do with this side skill than just teach classes at a karate school. Here, think outside the box, if you are in fact a karate instructor, you could write content about your experiences, you could sell eBooks on your website, perhaps you can create ten eBooks, imagine you sell over a million copies at $2.99 a ce? At this point, if you do reach this point, you will be venturing into million dollar status! Let's see, as a karate teacher, you could also offer online video classes to distant students. But before you do this, make sure to get good reviews from your former clients so that way your online community and the online world will have a sense of trust, when it comes to selling your particular brand, online buyers need a sense of trust established. Buyers have choices, and as a blogger, an entrepreneur, you always want to cater to your viewers more than your competitors.

Questions to ask yourself:

- What do I love to do in my free time?
- What interests me?
- What kinds of external and internal desires do I have?

- What do I enjoy researching?

- Simply put, is there anything particular that you are interested in?

- What do you like to read?

- What kind of content do you prefer to write?

- What kind of images do you like to see?

Choose a niche that solves your hearts woes, and begin to create your blog. Make sure to also plan out your blog posts. Next, plan an opening marketing strategy, target friends and family in their email, and target acquaintances or coworkers through social media. Let everyone know about the niche and blog you have chosen, this is a perfect time to get people interested in your blog. But before you launch anything, make sure that your launch has an utmost professional appearance. You will want to think of launch marketing strategies.

Blog Launch Marketing Strategies Include:

- Create a Facebook page that connects to your blog
- Create a nice email flyer on Illustrator or Photoshop
- Email family and friends
- Invite family and friends to your Facebook page, mention a link to your blog
- Connect your blog posts to your social media sites, every time you post on your blog, you will be able to spread the same post on to your connected social media sites

- Make sure your images pop with clarity and your content is error-free
- Pay Facebook and buy ad time, people will then hear about the launch of your blogging site while they browse on Facebook.
- You can also buy paid advertising on Twitter
- If you don't have a budget to work with, make daily posts and daily shares, this marketing method won't hurt, remember to reel in quality visitors only

Choosing a Proper Platform

Now let's drift our minds from niches to platforms. If you want to make some real money, this is the first and foremost step that you must take; retrieving a platform that allows you to manage all of your content. Decide to choose domains that allow you to monetize. Now, if you are utterly new to this, a domain is a .com. You want to be able to control the visitors and the incoming finances that are soon to be raking in. Don't opt to choose a free website, as you will limit the amount of capabilities you will have, choose to use a domain owned by you, you'll have much more abilities and capabilities as the administrator. There are websites such as fatcow.com which offer cheap prices to buy dot.coms, sometimes the start-up cost won't topple $100.00 for a whole entire year, that's doable. You are the blogger, the entrepreneur, don't let the third party website preparer take your advertising money, don't let third party corporations stunt your blogging growth, you are better than that. Of course, starting a blog isn't always free, but we recommend using Blogger (it's free), it's connected to the large IT player Google and Google Ads. Wordpress is good too, but in order to fully cap on full capabilities you'll need to pay an annual fee, the cost is under $500.00 U.S.D., and affordable. Although, if Blogger offers a free platform and you are struggling to start your blog, then free is a terrific option, choose Blogger. Blogger is more user friendly than Wordpress, but if you want to grow your blog in the future, you as a blogger will soon need to know the full technicality when it comes to Wordpress. WordPress is used by corporations and individuals all around and has built a good reputation over the years in the blogging world. Companies like The Huffington Post and Tech Crunch started the whole blogging trend, and now they are multi-millionaire companies! Just think of the indention that you as a blogger can make on society. Yes you can make a difference, but remember you must certainly blog with poise, noise, and keep it consistent. There are many platforms out there, just like there are many products out there on the market, every product and service claims they do all sorts of wonders, it's a selling tact. Always research the software that you will be downloading, or the service in which you will be using, and try to stick with the bigger name brand platforms, as there will be more credibility, reliability, and security that will be delivered to you and your blogging needs.

Trial and Error

If we want to succeed at anything in life we all have to fail at something in order to understand our past mistakes. In life, if we don't know something, chances are we might fail the first time, but if we do our very best to learn from the mistake and no longer implement the failed attempt strategy than we are bettering ourselves for future growth and advancement. Some of you are dealing with this circumstance, you started a blog, you post and then you get no feedback, no viewers, no nothing. Zilch, absolutely nothing! You have tried your hardest, but you just didn't seem to tap the right algorithm to allow you to become visible online. Stop experiencing error. How? By thinking through your strategies and by trying to make the best sound and logical decisions that you possibly can. If you are serious about making money from a blog, than it is highly advised that you start treating this like a responsible business. Before you begin full force, start accepting the challenges that you most likely will face. Always be positive about your new endeavor, *Making Money from Blogging,* and keep in mind that you are going to have to spend a lot of your own free time building your own blog if you want it to actually work. Glory doesn't come from being lazy. In order to succeed at *Making Money from Blogging,* you need to whip yourself into shape and you need to create, create, create! Now we will be absolutely clear about this particular piece of advice, creating just anything will absolutely not work! When you are writing, you need to make sure that you are creating content that matters! Content that has myriads of errors and that has very little thought will be found out sooner or later, so do yourself a favor and only create the very best, your very best! Remember, prestige will gain you higher rewards in the long-term, so please keep this in mind when learning how to *Make Money From Blogging*.

Focusing Fully On Content

Before you even begin to focus on blogging you need to make sure that you are focusing on creating quality content, otherwise you may risk losing a reader quickly and most certainly, if your content or visual images, or even advertisements, offend or bombard your viewers too much they might not ever visit your blog site again, now that would be an utter devastation! When we speak about quality content, we want to make sure that the content is error proof. But how do we go about knowing if it is error proof? The answer is easy and if you don't know it, than you might need to brush up on your skills. Simple, edit your work rigorously! Or have someone else edit your work for you, but keep in mind, eventually the editor will want to be paid. Hone, practice, and improve your editing skills. People all over the world will be reading your content and blog that you published, so keep it fresh, keep it clean in grammar, punctuation, and spelling. Every reader and viewer prefers a smooth and flowing type of read and a crisp image. By now, you should have already chosen your particular niche that you will concentrate on, so you can now focus on creating a lot of content, and by a lot, we mean, this is a consistent task that needs to be done on the daily. Plan out your publishing and posting schedule.

Set times and dates for yourself if you need to, in fact we highly recommend this strategy in order to keep you completely organized and on schedule. If you are not at the point where you can quit your day job just yet, than it is wise that you set aside certain times and days that you can write and concentrate on your blog. Creating an itinerary when it comes to strategizing your blogs success is most ideal. Even if you can only set aside two hours a night or two hours a week, you can make great progress on your blog. Make sure the content that you produce is pure quality content, we will keep mentioning this fact throughout our book, as it will throw any reader off, if your content is not up to par.

If you happen to be a poet, make sure that you have quality poetry, don't just slop just anything together, always put your best foot forward. If one blog idea doesn't work, learn to chalk it up, and move to another blog idea, don't just give up on your blog because it didn't work the first time. Make sure to practice and perfect your skills, otherwise your blog will remain stagnant, and what is a stagnant blog on the internet? A waste of space! Well those words are a little too harsh, so we take it back. We know, you worked hard on your blog thus far, so keep it up, but absolutely do not forget to market your blog on social media appropriately and affectivity. Otherwise there is a chance you could become invisible, as the masses will overshadow your glorious words waiting to be read. There are companies that started as blogs, Tech Crunch, and The Huffington Post, are a couple of examples. You should aspire to be like these companies, they are informative, highly followed, and now multi-millionaires. We are not necessarily saying to write in their particular niche or tone, but it may be wise to take a look at their sites, and recognize, when it comes to blogging, if you are good, consistent, well-liked, a good marketer, a good seller, and the list goes on, then you could in fact make it big

like The Huffington Post or Tech Crunch!

Meeting and Socializing With Other Bloggers

If you don't take time away from content producing and designing, then it is possible that you will set yourself up for failure. When you socialize on platforms that support other bloggers, it allows you the blogger to become more visible. Socializing and interacting with other bloggers allows bloggers all around to relate, unite, and come together and discuss. Discussion is important as the content will remain online and socializing will be sure to help you and blog get noticed. Get out there and socialize on your various blog websites, otherwise your blog could possibly suffer alienation. Being anti-social in the blogging world never gets anyone anywhere. Bloggers and creators always need other collaborators. Gain a good online reputation by providing quality work, ask to write on other blogs, and make sure that you always knock on doors, well, emails in this case. If you are writing with a journalistic approach, always back up your statements if resources are needed, otherwise you'll lose your journalistic credibility with readers. Always cite and link when appropriate, this can't be stressed enough. Never forget to cite your sources and quotations, this is an absolute imperative! Edit, edit, edit, all posts otherwise suffer being judged and thrown out!

The online market can be a cruel world, individuals all around do not see how quickly the internet is evolving, hence, why some individuals aren't selective when it comes to their online posts, don't be that person, and only post relevant information, that you strongly believe in, as the results will reap more rewards and get more reviews, comments, and insight. Controversy online works too for bloggers to gain in the ranks and views, but remember how populated our very own online system is, don't forget it is a dark-filled land of propaganda!

Be Sure To Download The WordPress Application on Your Smartphone

Since smartphones these days are so accessible to individuals all around, we recommend that you download the WordPress application. Downloading this application will help you keep up with blog posts on-the-go. Everyone has busy schedules, so what better way to keep up with your viewers and commentaries than with an application at hand! You can choose to be notified every time someone comments, pings back, or likes your posts; this will make it easier to connect with other bloggers and people simply looking to read. Connect at all times of the day and post whenever you feel like it! Of course, since we only recommend you post pure quality, if you are on-the-go and you don't have a pen, certainly jot down your idea in this application, but make sure to save your post as a draft, then later, when you have some quiet time to yourself, make sure that you go over your words, your images, your categories, and your tags, before finalizing the content that you will be publishing. Having the ability to manage your content and your social sites at the palm of your hand will keep you not only up-to-date, but it will keep you tuned in via real-time. This method will make sure that you are ready for the world of blogging. In fact, we recommend that you download all of the applications that you are currently using for your blog, download them on your smartphone, this will make sure that you can keep up with everything, including rapid random thoughts, social connections, and other bloggers.

Write For Other Bloggers

So we understand, you are not quite yet to the point of owning your own blogging business just yet, but you do have a blog that is established with daily followers, you have a nice portfolio, and a professional and clean looking template, so now is your time to reach out to other bloggers. Go online, research, and discover new and interesting blogs. Determine what kind of content and visualizations interest you. What do you like to look at? Determine who your competitors are and find niches that are similar to yours. Intently study.

Find more established links and write to the blog owner, but before you do, make sure that you grasp the tone of the actual blog before sending any pitches to the blog owner. Remember that first opinions are everything, these other bloggers, will only meet you online once, so you might as well make sure that you put your best blog foot forward, otherwise risk getting shunned early on in the game of online blogging. No one wants to be shunned, otherwise it will be harder to become visible online. Don't let your blog die out too early.

Keep in mind to always be nice and encouraging to other bloggers, they deal with the same obstacles that you have dealt with too, of course each blogger is always at a different stage in his or her career, after all it depends on the individual and their independent drive and motivation. You are the ultimate blogger, keep telling yourself that. Once you finally make online friends with popular and established bloggers, apply to posts on their blog, make sure you professionally contact them through their blog's contact page, and make sure you set up a pitch and an idea that actually has relevance to their page. Once you do this, send your pitch with poise, attach samples of work, links, and your biography, plus absolutely do not forget to add a contact email and phone number for the blogger to contact you back. Make it easy for them to find and browse your past work. Keyword, visibility.

Okay, finally another blogger recognizes your content and visualization skills, and invites you to guest blog on their page. Should you do it? The answer is easy, of course you should. The reasons? There are plenty of reasons. One, your writing will be seen, you might not get paid the first time when you get accepted to guest blog, but what will occur is that you will you become more visible, especially if you are guest blogging on a well-established blog that many people follow and read on a daily basis. So if you have an opportunity to guest blog, you'd better start blogging, as the more traffic that is linked to your blog, ultimately means more followers for your blog in the future.

Blogging takes time, and it takes time to gain traffic. If people don't have a clue about you, how do you think they will make it to your blog in the first place? You only have one chance when it comes to making a positive appearance on a guest blog, people judge quickly, so give them your raw soul, your love, your cold-blooded passion. Blogging is meant to be an internal release for some, enjoy what you do, help others, and share the love.

Analyzing Data, Visitors, etc.

When first deciding on your blog platform you need to be sure that you have a blogging platform that allows you to monetize your web earnings, if you don't do this in the beginning of your blog, than you could possibly lose out. We can't mention this enough, don't open a blogging account where the third party website limits your blogging abilities. We said this before, and we are going to say it again, as we see far too many good bloggers become tangled in this kind of web, their followers are enormous, but they are on a third party website, so the blogger ends up not getting paid for his or her marketing efforts on the ad side. Choose a site like Blogger, pay the premium for WordPress, or buy your own domain and map it to WordPress, but don't use a third party that doesn't allow you to monetize your earnings! Read the fine print before you agree and start publishing your content. There are many routes you can take, but never fall into the trap where you can't make money off of GoogleAd Words, or off of advertising in general. Some sites block monetizing, you as a new blogger, need to be aware of this fact. Don't fall into this scam and trap, we are warning you now!

When you are finally able to analyze the incoming traffic to your blog's site, you can start utilizing newly learned knowledge about the people who are following your blog, once you find useful information, make sure to cater to your visitor's needs.

Let us get one fact straight, in the world of blogging, traffic and visitors are the blood of blogging. If traffic doesn't run through the bloggers pages and veins then there would be no heart beating blog, your blog would simply be dead. Keep your visitors satiated at all times! Once you are able to learn the art of this, money will be running in, whether you like it or not.

Monetizing Your Site

Now this is the whole entire reason as to why we are reading this particular book, now let's get into the nuts and bolts about, *Making Money from Blogging,* Ah what is monetizing? If you don't know about monetizing than get out of here and stop reading this now! No, in all seriousness, this is why we are here, monetizing is why we are here. We are here of course because we want to have the ability to work on our own time, and to have access and freedom to uncapped monetary gains, that is why we are here in the first place.

Ways To Monetize Your Blog Include (Short Version):

- Advertising (Google Adwords & Adsense)

- Amazon (affiliate marketing)

- EBooks

- Webinars (paid) Online Classes

- Services

- Advertisements, Private Companies

- Products

- Videos

- Audio

- Content

Adding EBooks, Products, and Services to Your Blog

You can add ads onto your blog page and let your blog complacently sit online, of course that would be a complete newbie approach, don't do that! An entrepreneur who usually succeeds always diversifies their portfolio, and you know what this causes? This causes an influx of more streams of income. EBooks these days sell! There are notable online EBook sellers that have been known to hit it big and sell millions of copies, all from solely advertising online, eBooks have become a trend.

EBooks have changed the way that we read, of course, this is because of the edge and growth technology has seen, but because of this fact, we can now begin to realize how many paths there are, when it comes to seeking out different ways to make money online! Adding other products onto your blogging site, after your readers trust you (of course), is ideal, because not only will this allow you to gain income, it will allow you to continue your business. Incoming money will keep your blogging business thriving. Always be weary upon what you directly advocate for. If it doesn't feel right, it's probably not.

Connect To All External Links

Connecting your blog to an external link should be implemented because the more links that you direct to your blog, the higher rating your traffic will be. And let's get this straight, in the blogging world, traffic really is everything. Advertising is also a big revenue source when it comes to blogging so link, link, link, and don't you start to think twice.

Using Ads and Videos

Using ads and videos will make sure that you are gaining viewers. People, well, the masses anyway, the masses love images! You always want to capture your readers with interesting imagery as this will immediately catch their attention, catching the attention of the masses will put your blog on the forefront.

If you do use videos, we always highly suggest that you use YouTube, or some kind of video platform system that actually lets you monetize your earnings through viewers watched and ads played. Using eye catching media will be sure to catch your audience in a glimpse of a second. Snap! But also we aware, that initial glance appearance is your first objective. You want to basically position yourself at a stance where not only is your content visually intriguing, but your content is complete quality, also your headline has to be a clickable attention-getter! If no one understands what you will be talking about in your blog post, than why would they be interested, when it comes to reading your content in the first place? That just is not happening! Impress your readers with lively content!

Gain Quality Audience, Rather Than Quantity

A main reason to choose a quality audience to read your content is because quality lasts for the long-term, bad quality equals visitors that don't return to your blogging site. Yes, in the analytics sense, we look at the quality of visitors that attend your page each day too. Pay attention to this, because over time, knowing more about your audience will empower you as a blogger. Download Google Analytics and follow the instructions to see your blogs rank.

Know what kind of audience you are reaching. Gaining quality visits takes time, trust, loyalty, and somewhat of a platonic online friendship. If you want great visitors you have to treat your traffic great and provide them with quality, if you expect to get quality in return, you'd better dish it out. The universe gives what it gets.

Maintaining Your Blog

Maintaining your blog is a whole new story, now of course as we have been mentioning, this takes a lot of hard driven sweat! Driven sweat, meaning you will be spending most of your hours blogging. Think of it this way, your friends that work the normal nine to five, they will be begging you to hang out and socialize with them, meanwhile, if you leave your computer for one second, than other bloggers will in fact rise to the top first! Don't let peer pressure reel you in from achieving your well sought out blogging dreams and goals.

Blogging is an extremely competitive market, so the moment that you drift off task, the moment that you step away from your computer, and take your hands off of your computer, is the moment where all of your future slips away. Just kidding, as a blogger, learn how to balance your work/life schedule. Yes, blogging is competitive, this fact won't change, but tackle this feat, if you really want it, you can do it! If you want to become an extremely serious blogger than it should be in your best interest to always write, write, write, and publish! But remember to publish with style, quality, and intent. Otherwise all of your readers will think that you are utterly incompetent. Who wants to be known as the 'incompetent blogger'? Word will get around and perhaps you'll get page views, but let's get real, the page views won't be considered quality followers if you damage you bloggers reputation and site by publishing incoherent words with tons of editing mistakes, that is exactly what your page viewers will take away. Don't ruin yourself and always publish wisely.

Headlines Are Crucial!

Everyone knows that not one person in their right mind will click on a title headline if they have no clue what it is about. When writing your blogging post headlines, you need to make sure that you choose an attention-getter headline. You need to choose a headline that is relevant to your blog post. Now that we are mentioning headlines, we can now begin to explore headlines more in depth. In order to understand headlines in a more intricate sense, we need to venture out, and research trends. In case you are new to trends, let's talk about trends, it is actually easier to find trends than you think.

Thanks to the advanced and easily accessible internet, we can find trends on social media sites such as: Facebook, Twitter, Instagram, Google, you name it, if you begin to research trends on these sites, chances are you'll find the answer to your question in a matter of seconds, with a simple search titled 'trends'. Now if you want to go deeper, which you should want to, as knowledge is power, (if we have no clue about ways to enhance our blogs earnings, then really, what is the point?). Studying trends can be an interesting experience, because when you get deeper into the research, you will be able to see that there really is no pattern when it comes to trends in the making, trends happen because of various reasons. Usually popularity inside of a trend will hit hard and then die down rather rapidly, with a new trend arising shortly after. Keeping up with daily trends will continue to give you an edge as a blogger. Every single day, make sure to set a time aside so that way you can research and study past and current trends. If you can make your content relevant to the times in 2016 and so on, and provide a quality read, visitors will be flocking to your blog site. Also shares and likes will become the normalcy. It is important to implement this task on a daily basis, as trends go in and out. Research!

Edit, Edit, Edit

Blogging, the only reason we are going to consistently stuff this advice in this book, *Making Money from Blogging,* is because blogging is mainly about content and visuals. Readers and audience love entertainment. Entertainment is what keeps our human lives interesting. Editing our content will continue to show our readers that we are serious about our blog and that we are serious about considering our blog a business. The keywords that exemplify blogging are, professionalism, having an edge, and learning how to connect to an online community of people.

SEO Keywords, Utmost Importance

SEO content and keywords, what is this? Well, to make things simple, SEO stands for search engine optimization. We all should be aware that Google is not only a global player, but an extremely useful tool when it comes to online searching and content. Using Google and working in unison with Google, will ensure that your blogging website and business grows. Make sure to add SEO content into your blogging site, in other words, make sure that your content is density rich in keyword content, by at least 45-55%, if you want to eventually become visible online. An example, say your blog content is about medicine and the human spine, well, you'd better make sure that you decide on keywords and flood your content with the keywords that you choose, this will help your content be found online. In this case, you can use keywords such as: 'human spine' and 'medicine'.

WordPress

If you are a blogger, than it is wise that you know how to use WordPress, you need to be able to be technically savvy; otherwise the next blogger will be read and followed over you! Don't limit yourself, by not learning the proper technical skills and information that you need to learn to complete a professional looking blog. WordPress started in the year, 2003 as a C.M.S based company, a content management system. WordPress is used as a professional source to share content, utilize all of the blogging tools out there. We most certainly recommend signing up with wordpress.com.

Blogger

Blogger is another platform that is useful for all bloggers around. Keep in mind when blogging, it is never useful to only use one platform, publish, spread your content, link it, and connect it to your original site, if you really want to optimize the amount of viewers that you have and will soon gain. A little background information about Blogger, Blogger is actually connected to Google Adsense, remember this, we've mentioned it twice, so if you are immediately looking to monetize your blog earnings, than it is incredibly wise that you initially start with Blogger, since Blogger works hand and hand with Google Adsense.

Facebook

Facebook, ah Facebook, the glory of social media and connecting to one another. With Facebook we are now able to communicate on a grand and global level. Staying in touch across the globe has never been so easy. When you begin your blogging career, you also need to make sure that you publish, and you share your quality blog posts on your online social media site, Facebook. Otherwise, how will your peers and future readers know that you even exist? Don't just sit around and expect people to knock on your door, you gotta pound the pavement, and knock away at doors, yes, that is right, you are the blogger, you want to be read? So you have to be the knocker. Facebook is a great tool to market your blogging content to your friends and family. Let's say that you have one thousand friends on your friend list, your other friend has three thousand; technically speaking, if you convince your friend to share your latest blog post, your new market reach would now be four thousand people, and the numbers will continue to increase upon how many shares the blog post gets. Post, share, and like, these are pertinent in the world of online blogging. This step will ultimately lead you to monetary success; don't forget, the more money in your pocket, the sooner you are to your lavish retirement.

- **Rules to follow on Facebook:**
- First and foremost, realize that Facebook is much more of a personal site rather than Twitter, LinkedIn, etc. On Facebook, sure sometimes we have our work associates, but we also have our friends and family, make sure to post away

- Don't over post as you could irritate your readers

- Watch how the diction in your content is exerted

- Keep your tone warm and friendly

LinkedIn

No one really thinks about LinkedIn when it comes to blogging, but what some bloggers are missing out on is the ability to reach a bigger and bigger audience, you are darn right, our advice is to post your blogging links on LinkedIn. Of course every site has its own etiquette, so make sure you follow the proper etiquette when posting on any site, being aware of this factor, will only help you, before you make a detrimental posting mistake that likely causes you trouble or less traffic down the road. Okay, enough, onto positivity, what bloggers miss is that if you are a member of LinkedIn, you have the ability to follow and join certain groups, you can choose related niches to follow, simply by the stroke of a proper keyword search, which can then lead you to a plethora of an entire horizon of a whole new network! Post gracefully and wisely, yet remember, LinkedIn, is not like Twitter or Facebook, LinkedIn, is one of its own, and is a social platform site directed at connecting business professionals all around the world. So be sure to complete your profile and make sure that you provide one simple, clean, and professionally looking photo. Publish relevant blog information on LinkedIn occasionally, too much is never good, especially on LinkedIn.

Twitter

So many social media sites exist in the year 2016. Twitter offers another route for bloggers.

Twitter is different than Facebook as Twitter is known to be less personal and more for business alerts. Twitter allows a way for users to share information globally with a short amount of characters, (words). Say something concise and brief, yet get your point across is the entire feel. Twitter is a good way to share blog links, it is a great way to gain an audience of followers that you can eventually link back to your blog site, in turn gaining you quality visitors that actual visit your blog site because they actually get something in return from your site, whether it is advice or some kind of tangible item. If your visitors are receiving something great, they will be satiated. More traffic equals more money for the blogger. Add your blog website to your Twitter profile, anyone and everyone can now have access to your blog, so as long as you are okay with this fact, then everything should be green and ready to go.

Rules to follow on Twitter:

- Be concise

- Post relevancy only

- Don't over post

- Reblog other Twitter users

- Communicate in a friendly yet professional way with other users

- Be mindful of the words you post

- Add images as this will increase your chances of receiving more viewers/traffic

- You need to have killer headlines!! (Utmost important!)

- Like other posts, be sociable, and welcoming if you want more followers

- Keep in mind, more followers on Twitter, will mean more visibility for your ever so precious blog that you have created.

The Importance of Widgets

Have you ever been reading a blog and you loved it so much that you wanted to share this wonderful and new blog post, but sadly you were unable to because there were no share buttons? The share buttons or the reblog buttons were non-existent, which then limited you, preventing you from re blogging the great and fabulous Author whom you just discovered. Sadly the Author could have had many more followers once you reblogged the glorious piece of art. This particular Artist limited themselves, by not adding widgets onto their blog site. Always add social share widgets to each blog post! Why wouldn't you?

Hone Your Creativity

When we say hone your creativity what we really mean, is hustle your way to more cash flow! You need to tap into the creative you and you need to be able to create and think of various ways in which you can rake in more dough. You need to stretch your arms out to various paths. Choosing one path in the blogging world isn't all that smart. When we mention paths, we want you to start thinking more and more outside of the box as we've been mentioning. You need to be able to not only blog on your blogging website, but you need to get creative and start offering more things on your site that will lead to financial gain.

Let's talk more in depth about paths, we need to offer our visitors: eBooks, products, services, or advertising; this is where the mula really comes from. Say you are a financial consultant, not only can you sell financial services on your website blog, but you can jump outside of the box and start to create quality eBooks that offer financial consulting, your traffic will love this, if it is well written. Of course, create a strategy before you even begin to start. An example strategy would be, offering your visitors a free and valuable eBook for their pure enjoyment. Your blog visitors will love you for this mere gesture and they will surely come back to visit your site, but the next time they do, you as the blogger should upload your newly written eBook, this time charge for it. Chances are if your visitors loved your first free eBook, your teaser, chances are, they will take a chance, and buy your second book. The free giveaway strategy always makes visitors feel appreciated and of course people want to come back if they feel like someone is actually appreciating them and solving their problems at the same time. There are many ways to monetize a blog, so don't forget this fact.

Promotional giveaways also prove to help your service, product, or business, why? Well, the answer is easy, if you offer a limited amount of something to the public, and it is in fact a quality product or service, well then, word will travel, and reviews will flood in. Start thinking about giving back to people, before you start thinking about how you will rake in more cash. If you are too concentrated on the cash at hand, you will not be providing your visitors with ultimate results, as you will be too concerned on receiving than giving, this is never good. Do not fall into this trap when you become a blogger, otherwise risk losing visitors early on.

Strategize Your Marketing Efforts

If you are wanting to switch your nine to five mundane life schedule into a full blown online blogger then get ready to market your entire efforts away, day in and day out. Marketing isn't such a breezy process as it is an absolute time guzzler. The only way to market, is to consistently reach out and tell the world about your blog, product, service, giveaway, your brand, etc., you have to be vocal when it comes to communication and being a blogger. Marketing is important, not only is the actual process of marketing necessary, this is an ongoing and never ending implementation. Next up, is analyzation. Set-up a plan to know the numbers. Know viewer traffic numbers in order to assess and analyze trends on certain days, certain times, and years, etc. Learn about the demographic population that you are reaching. Ask yourself questions such as; what types of demographics do you want to reach? What age group? Region? All of these questions are helpful to know because if you study your viewers, chances are you will be able to solve their needs, rather than if you didn't know anything about them. How will you solve your viewer's needs? This is especially important. Once you know what your niche is, and once you have a good amount of posts that are of course, a hand crafted piece of quality nature, then you can begin your marketing endeavors. Although marketing endeavors go a long way, if sales numbers and financials are not coming in, then we can classify marketing efforts as ineffective and defective. Always strategize appropriately. Write down your blogger's business plan.

Analyzation Strategies

- **Google Analytics (suggested)**

Abilities include: Viewing demographic and region data, viewing the amount of visitors per day, including data regarding exact time, location, gender, age, etc.; this marketing data can be retrieved from an awesome platform provided from one of the top players in the IT sector, Google! Maximize the tools that have been freely handed to you. Google offers us great free tools, now utilize Google and Blogger. You may be asking yourself, what exactly will you be doing with the information that you are retrieving? You can simply use the data to improve your viewer's experience, that is one thing you can do as a blogger, you can also use this data, to make sure that you are hitting your target goals. Hitting your target goals, will ensure that you keep rising the ladder. Once you download Google Analytics and you are able to view your tangible traffic, you can then start to realize that *Making Money from Blogging* is actually possible.

Sales

Okay, so your marketing skills worked and you now have a few sales, whether it is from your posted eBook, a client emailed you to provide services for them, a visitor buys your product, or your film and video sell, whatever the sale, you need to be able to keep up with the sales department. Always keep in mind that marketing and sales go hand-in-hand. In order for anyone to know about what you do or what your intention is, they need to be impressed with the image and the brand, before looking further. Once you catch your visitors with intent, and a way to solve their problem, you can then reel them in with a quality and a unique type of voice. Before you start posting your products and or services, you as the blogger, need to tap into the entrepreneur side of your soul. Tapping into your business side, you need to start researching industry rates and pricing, decide on your pricing strategy before you begin, and stick to it. Don't limit yourself and accept rates that clearly are low ball rates, have dignity and patience, and seek for quality clients. Here is some great advice, you exert quality, well in a world full of karma, a boomerang of quality is bound to come back to the striving blogger, as long as pure determination is shown. Sales is a numbers game and can be very frustrating for some. Being a professional blogger, who actually makes money off of blogging doesn't just require content skills; this requires a vast amount of different skills, in order for the blogger to survive in the competitive world of blogging. Hone various skills.

Rinse and Repeat

Blogging is an ongoing process, once you start, once you light a fire with your fuel (your blogging content), and once you gain a momentum with your daily, weekly, monthly, and yearly visitors you can't stop blogging, this is a process that must be rinsed and repeated with a non-stop attitude, day by day. Sound too grueling? Now is your chance to drop-out, but we are just giving the realistic facts here in the year 2016. Perhaps one day you will outgrow your blog, as you will have surpassed all of the goals that you set out for your blog to accomplish? At this point in your blogging career, you are making so much money from in, it pays for itself, all you do is post blogging content, and it pays. Perhaps you don't feel like posting every single day anymore, perhaps the years have passed and you are now in an authoritative stance and position. At this point, you can then use a strategy of using the profit earned, and pay other writers to write future content for you. Of course you need proper and qualified applicants; otherwise you risk poor blogging content. But don't worry as everything needs to be approved before being published, and approval must be granted by the CEO of course, and in this case, the CEO is now you. Choose quailed writers to help you out when it comes to writing your blogging content, this couldn't be such a bad idea. Qualified meaning, a rad portfolio with an accredited college degree, plus experience. Yes, you as a business owner will be paying a staff of writers to write quality blogging posts, but as long as the viewers continue to rake in, you are still making money. Make a point to bring in more profit than you are spending, this will surely keep you on a path built with financial security and success, *Making Money From Blogging* is real, it is actual and factual!

If you eventually work yourself up to this opportunity and position, then it is wise if you spend and keep track of your finances wisely, you will need a bookkeeper and an accountant at this point. Choose whether or not blogging is your path. Once you get to this point in your blogging career, you'll be able to choose whether or not you want to work remotely and control a staff of bloggers that you hire, while you are enjoying yourself traveling the entire globe. Or you can choose to simply relax and manage your team all from the comfort of your home near a creek. Mind you, once your blogging site prevails with millions of visitors each day, you will be able to pay off your entire mortgage in one shot, so keep at it. When you are a successful blogger, you can choose your destiny, you are no longer, what we consider, 'corporate capped'. You as a blogger and a freelance entrepreneur have an opportunity for limitless possibilities, these possibilities will allow you to make maximum profit. The sky really is the limit in this case, as the sales, and blogging efforts are all up to you, you are the boss, so tread with a fierce and competitive force in the blogging world. Speak loudly, have dignity, gain respect, and provide knowledge, solutions, and a helping hand, to your blogging community and all around. Your work and the effort you put into it doesn't represent a company or a corporation, the amount of work that you provide for your blog, your brand, will in turn reflect a large amount on you, the blog owner.

Staying In-The-Know

As stated, there is no set formula when it comes to blogging, but following the above advice will surely help any blogger get set and ready to head onto a journey of blogging. Blogging can be a hit or miss when it comes to choosing a proper domain title, realize when one of your sites clearly just doesn't work out, just let it go, bite the bullet, and just create another one. Once you love your niche to a point where you do not hate what you are doing, can you then begin to flourish as an actual blogger. Since there is really no particular formula to follow in the art of blogging, every successful blogger needs to be a cutthroat hustler, otherwise other bloggers will be preferred. This is a scary thought for every individual blogger; of course you want the attention to veer towards your blogging site, not the other blogger! In order to outdo your competition you need to constantly be reading, day and night, don't just concentrate on creating massive amounts of content. Your viewers don't want to be flooded, in fact they want to see miracles and beautiful posts, not sloppy junk that hits their screens and eventually makes them cringe. Don't be out of your mind! The annoying marketing strategy doesn't work when we are striving for quality.

If you have the opportunity and the means to do it, it would be wise to take design classes, as this skill can help you as a blogger learn important tools. Learn software such as: Photoshop, Illustrator, Adobe Suite, etc. knowing more, will place you in an advantageous spot in the online world. You don't need to spend an arm and a leg when it comes to taking these classes, but it would be beneficial for you, especially if you don't know the basics, of Photoshop or Illustrator. Viewers love graphics, and if you have original photography, your photo can always pop more if you edit it on a software such as, Illustrator or Photoshop. Popping and crisp looking images that satisfy the reader's eyes will prove more and more traffic over time. You'd better be advertising crisp images on your blog at this point, that is, if you are in fact receiving a lot of traffic, otherwise you could be cutting yourself short.

Things to remember:

- Continuously educate yourself
- Learn new systems and software as it emerges, this will only help you, the blogger

- Attend workshops and seminars, you don't necessary need a full-blown college degree to be a blogger, of course, we recommended college, as a Bachelor's degree rounds the mind and proves to help every individual look outside-of-the-box, especially in western nations.
- Read and research basically until your eyes fall out
- Keep these words at the surface of your brain, "you'll always be a student, learning your entire life, the world is vast, and the knowledge inside is infinite, learning is growth."
- We cannot stress this enough, quality over quantity posts only!

Keep Your Head Above Water, Know What to Do If Your Blog Is Not Succeeding

Of course, we are not telling you to quit your full-time job that pays your bills, especially if you have a family to care for and to feed. It is best that when any business owner starts any new business that they make sure they have funds stocked away in case there is an emergency that unfortunately arises. We always need to keep safety funds in our accounts. When you start a blog and you decide that you want to leave your nine to five job, you need to make sure that you have enough funds to tide you over for at least six months. The beginning is always the toughest period. We consider this the breakout period, which in this case, you want to be striving and performing at your maximum, so be like Nike and 'just do it'! Every blogger needs to build his or her audience. Content building and blogging is a process, a process that involves continuous tender love and care. But let's face the truth, if you really love what you do, and you chose a niche that interests you the most, plus you're making a regular and decent income, what do you have to complain about? Yes, nothing in life is perfect, this is true, but when it comes time for blogging, or better yet any endeavor that we set our hearts on, practice really does make perfect. Ongoing efforts and full devoted time will surely outdo competitors that are on their blogging game, 'every now and then'. A devoted blogger is a strong quality blogger, waiting to burst out into full succession, you'll get there.

If you need a part-time job while you build-up your audience, well then get one, there is no shame in working more hours, especially if you need a paycheck, don't acquire debt, you'll hold yourself back in life. Until blogging has proven to pay your bills and then some, can you then begin to call it a full-time job. If you are not making enough money, and can barely keep your head afloat, and you are drowning in bills, make the logical decision and get a part-time job while you begin to build you blogging empire. Blog every single day, converse, and send out those well-written proposals. Stay consistent, offer something to the universe and soon the universe will be bound to give back to you, the striving and helpful blogger.

Job Boards and Proposals

Luckily the internet is so vast, as this fact allows us to have unlimited opportunities when it comes to online knowledge and monetary gains. If you are a freelance blogger, you can find jobs on sites like ProBlogger.com, the jobs posted on this site offer opportunities for bloggers to find paid jobs that actually pay the blogger per post. Learn to write convincing proposals in order to reel new clients in. You'd better not have one minuscule mistake in your proposal content, otherwise you will risk looking like a complete fool, and you better believe you most likely will not receive a response, and if you receive any kind of response, chances are the job poster will correct you proposal mistakes. When it comes to spelling, grammar, and punctuation, you never want to throw off your reading audience simply by disrupting the flow.

Massacre's Regarding Blogger's, Current Events

Recently there has been reports of blogger's being attacked by extremist religious groups, these groups are threatening bloggers, and have even carried out actual killings among blogger's. Apparently extremist religious groups have carried out attacks and have justified their reasoning by saying the blogger was defaming an actual religion. Blogger's everywhere have a right to exercise freedom of speech, but as our internet grows, and cyber war continues, blogger's be alert. An American born blogger just recently has been hacked to death in Bangladesh, 2016. The motive? An extremist religious belief thought that the blogger was creating blasphemy, hence why they hacked him to death. Bangladesh has recently received media, stating that their country is changing due to an influx of extremist religious beliefs. The story is still evolving, to read more about this blogger tragedy, please see CNN.com for more information.[1] As we get deeper into the cyber war that we are currently in, in the year 2016, we as bloggers need to stand strong with our free thinking, freedom of speech ideologies, we should maintain to keep. But we also need to be more vigilant, as a cyber war has sprung, whether anyone wants to announce it or not. Be the change, and offer glorious and helpful information. Do not be the blogger that offers corrupt information, otherwise legal suits could rise, or inciting violence is also another occurrence that could take place.

---

[1] http://www.cnn.com/2016/06/20/asia/bangladesh-avijit-roy-suspect-killed/

Sure we should feel comfortable, being that our first amendment protects us as law abiding citizens with freedom of speech, but as we read this news story case, a free-thinker blogger who lived in a predominantly religious country, was hacked for speaking his mind? This resonates deeply with us, be careful how you write, but speak up, and speak enlightenment, as good shall always prevail. By no means, shall self-expression equal fatality. To have such an ideology is monstrous. Blogger's all around, try to write from all sides of the story; neutrality is rather appealing to readers, as you tend to keep a sense of mystery. And who does not like mystery? Not us. Blog on!

Never Give Up Blogging

If blogging is a passion of yours and you've never made any money off of blogging, then it is likely that you didn't want to make money off of blogging in the first place. But if you dig deeper and place yourself in an entrepreneur and business mind stance, you can then begin to see profits and revenue flowing in. And don't you dare forget, blogging is not about one sole website, you must connect many links, products, and offerings, to your site in order for traffic to increase and come back to your site. Help your readers trust your site, and soon they will purchase anything on your site. If your true heart is set on telling the world how you feel, well then we advise that you do so, if you want to be an advocate and a journalist, by all means, be one. But if you do in fact choose the journalistic approach through your blogging site, make sure that you report only truth, and cite appropriately or you could very well end up with a slapped wrist and a law suit in the waiting. The internet has changed the way in which we conduct business, there are many litigation cases that are currently open regarding blogger's and accusations of slander and defamation, so be careful what you say in the year 2016. Remember, in journalism, you should be reporting just the facts anyway, read the law, on journalism, simply with a quick search on Google. Here in the United States, we are protected with our first amendment freedom of speech, but report with intent, truth, and dignity.

Thank you for reading and best of luck to you and your blog!

Online Startups

How to Start a Business

And Make Money as an

Online Coach

T. Whitmore

TABLE OF CONTENTS

Introduction

How to build an online coaching business and not just have a job as a coach

How to think to make maximum money as an online coach

How to build reputation as a starting online coach

What will you be known for as an online coach?

What you sell as an online coach is not what people buy

How to exercise control over clients

Mistakes to avoid in client relationships

How to price your online coaching services

Conclusion

INTRODUCTION

In this book we will cover everything you need to know about online coaching.

Most online coaches approach their profession wrong. They chase clients. They try to sell coaching services at low prices. When they do, they have no control over their clients and they have terrible retention in their coaching programs.

This book will explain to you how you can avoid all these mistakes and build an actual coaching business.

If you want to be a successful online coach, you need to think and approach this business in a certain way. You want to be able attract clients instead of chasing them. You want to get clients that will do what you tell them to do. You want to charge premium prices and not deal with clients who nickel-and-dime you.

To be able to do so, you need to think in a certain way and approach the business of online coaching in a certain way.

We will start this book with discussing the differences between an online coaching business and a job as a coach. We will then talk about how you need to think to make good money as an online coach.

All successful online coaches are known for something. They have a certain kind of reputation. Building a reputation from scratch is what we will cover next.

Online coaching is not just about providing advice. It is about exercising control over clients, making sure that they are happy and that they are getting value the way they define value. We will talk about all of this in the chapter called "What you sell as an online coach is not what people buy."

Finally, we will cover the subjects of mistakes to avoid and of getting paid.

The information that you will learn from this book works in any industry with any size of business.

It works if you are a health coach and work with clients one-on-one. It also works if you want to coach freelancers or entrepreneurs who have a few people working for them. You can also apply strategies and information from this book to work with big corporations.

The thing you need to understand about b2b or business-to-business selling is that there is no such thing. Businesses do not buy anything. People buy everything.

If you are selling to consumers, your consumers usually have just one question about your product or service: "Is this for me?" They may wonder about pricing, alternatives and other issues, but fundamentally they are trying to figure out if the product or service is for them.

Selling to businesses is more complicated. A business buyer is trying to answer two questions. The first one is very similar to the consumer one:

1. Is this for my organization?

A business buyer usually has another question. He or she is also trying to figure out where they are in this deal. A product or service may be a great fit for their organization, but politically within the organization they can't make a buying decision at this moment. This question is similar to

2. If my organization buys it, will this be good for me personally?

This is it. When selling to consumers there is one major question, when selling to businesses there are two. Everything else is the same.

When selling to businesses, you are still selling to people who have feelings and emotions and make decisions in the same way your other customers do. The numbers change. The strategies and principles don't.

What you will often think when reading this book is the following: "This sounds great, but my business is different. This may work for a coach in X, but it won't work for me."

Such thoughts are never helpful. It's always self-sabotage. Finding reasons why something can't work or won't work isn't a high-paid job.

Any janitor, any taxi driver, any McDonald's employee, any low-wage worker can come up with reasons why they are not employed at a job that is paying a lot. Finding excuses is never hard.

What is harder and what is the key to money and wealth, is figuring out how something applies to you, your situation, and your business. That's what you always want to be doing.

You also need to throw out the idea that you need formal education or some other qualifications from some institution to be a successful online coach.

Do you know where Dr. Phil went to school? What about Tony Robbins? What about Gary Vaynerchuk or Grant Cordone? You probably don't. Truth is, the marketplace doesn't care. All formal requirements are the blocks that you have in your head. They are not real blocks to success as an online coach.

HOW TO BUILD AN ONLINE COACHING BUSINESS AND NOT JUST HAVE A JOB AS A COACH

If you go to some version of a Coaching Institute or a Coaching School or a Coaching Certification Program, if you spend some time listing to a group of speakers from the National Speakers Association, you will find dollars-for-hours culture. People will be discussing charging $50 per hour, going from $50 per hour to $100 per hour and so on.

The entire culture is going to be about exchanging time for money.

There are several problems with that.

The first problem is that your time is finite. Even if you find a way to work 24 hours a day as coach at $50/hour, you will still only be making $1200/day and there will be no way for you to make more because your time is limited.

When there is no way to make more, no future, no progress, no advancement, people usually get bored in any job. Sooner or later it happens with everyone.

Ultimately, every lawyer that charges per hour, every psychologist, every CPA does not want to be a lawyer or a psychologist or a CPA. They feel stuck and that's what will happen to you, too, if you charge per hour.

Therefore, it is impossible to make serious money by charging per hour and it's also impossible to make significant progress.

The second problem with charging per hour is that it's not really a business. It is a job that has no leverage. It has no multiplier effect.

In this book we will be talking about online coaching as a business where you can charge not per hour, but per project or per value that you deliver to a client.

Here's how you want to be thinking about coaching and the value a coach provides: If you go to a therapist who saves a marriage, how much is it worth? How much do two people save by not going through a divorce and not having their lives turned upside down?

You never want to be comparing a coach to some worker who is getting paid hourly. You always want to be looking at a bigger picture, because you will be able to charge more and you will be able to help people get what they want.

Nobody hires a coach because they want to spend $X/hour on a coach. People hire a coach, a therapist, a business consultant because they want to accomplish certain results. That's what you want to be talking about, that's what you want to be looking at when pricing your services.

Another reason not to charge per hour is very simple: when you charge per hour, everyone is unhappy.

We discussed above why you will be unhappy. Your clients are also going to be unhappy. They will feel like they are overpaying because they will be viewing your services as an exchange of dollars for minutes of your time if you allow them to do so by advertising your services as hourly based.

They will be talking to you and thinking: "I am paying this guy $500 per hour and we already talked for 30 minutes. I just spent $250. Was there enough value for me in those 30 minutes to justify paying $250?"

That's what will happen if you charge hourly and not based on "saving a marriage."

To become a successful coach, you simply need to get rid of this traditional thinking in as many ways as you can.

How do you charge for coaching, then?

One of the examples is cash above base. Let me explain how that works. You sit down with a client and say: "Okay, how much did you do last year?"

Let's assume that your prospective client earned $100,000 for the simplicity of the argument. Let's assume that the rate of inflation is 10% and growth rate of the business is another 10%.

This means that this year without your help and everything going the way this prospective client has been doing in the past, he or she will make $120,000. This will be the base for the first year.

The base for the second year will be calculated in the same manner. Let's say it's $140,000 for the second year and $168,000 for the third year.

As a coach you could promise that you will help to grow the business and for your compensation you want 30% of all the money that business makes above the numbers outlined above.

Then you could convince someone that you are really good and you could take the business to $500,000 the first year. It means that you will get one third of (500-120)/3 = $125,000.

You can then discount that by convincing your prospective client to giving you, say, $10,000 of this money upfront.

The numbers in this example aren't very important. What's important is that we've just showed you how you can get away from discussing hours for dollars in the coaching business. What you are now going to deliver in this scenario is irrelevant. Your customers can't start counting minutes figuring out if they are paying you too much per minute. The only thing that is relevant in the coaching program described above is the growth of the business.

The second thing that most Coaching Universities obsess about is formal training.

This is easy to understand, because formal training is what they are selling. They are all hung up about qualifications and education and credentials and alphabet soup after a name. They will tell you that you can't do business as an online coach without those letters after your name. In reality, this has nothing in common with the truth.

It is extremely important to understand that nobody cares about the letters after your name except for institutions selling you the letters and people who have already bought the letters.

The marketplace doesn't care. Today we live in a celebrity-driven culture, not in an expertise-driven culture.

Schooled experts were making really good money 30 or 40 years ago. People that are making really good money today are celebrities.

Here's a practical example for you that will perfectly demonstrate this.

If you have two fitness coaches and one has a degree from Harvard and all the alphabet letters after his or her name you can think of and the other one is a coach for Kim Kardashian, more people today would choose the Kim Kardashian guy versus the Harvard guy.

Formal training misconceptions also reflect in ladder thinking. Now, ladder thinking is very important because that's how you want all the people around you to think.

When we grow up, it is our parents who decide when we are old enough to babysit our siblings, choose our own clothes, date. Then we go to school where there are grades and one can't go to grade five after grade two.

The only way to go is one, two, three and so on. It's a ladder.

Ladders surround us everywhere in life. We grow up conditioned to think in terms of ladders.

Truth is, climbing up the ladders is not how life works for most successful people. Bill Gates, Mark Zuckerberg, Steve Jobs dropped out of college. They did not wait until they were done climbing the ladder and graduating.

Also, nobody appointed them to start their businesses.

They've done so, because they've decided to do it.

This is a template for you to follow:

Stop climbing ladders created by other people.

Do the things you decide to do, when you decide to do them

At the same time, you do not want to try and change the thinking of people around you. Having someone change the way they think is hard, ungrateful work. That's not the work you want to be doing.

Therefore, the formula to success as an online coach is the following:

Don't climb ladders built by others; build your own ladders for people to climb.

You want to be sticking ladders in front of your prospects and clients. And once they do climb a ladder, you want to stick another one right in front of them, because they will climb it.

That's what we all have been conditioned to do.

At the same time it's very important for you to never climb one.

When someone shows you a ladder, you should laugh at it.

You've got to realize that a bunch of people like you sat down in a room and figured out how to build yet another ladder.

Boy Scouts of America has a ladder. A number of people got together in a room and figured out how to build one so that they could control kids and their parents. There's no other reason for that ladder to be there.

A warning: when you do get all the Coach University Certification Thinking out of your head, people from Coach University are not going to be happy about it.

People around you who keep charging dollars per hours are not going to be happy about you making more money than they are making, either.

How dare you charge this kind of money?

That's what you will be hearing from them and that's how you know that you are doing something right.

There is a continuous conversation in the American society about the ratio between the regular Joy the worker pay and the CEO pay. A lot of people find it very unfair that a CEO can be making 100x, 1000x, 10000x what the lowest paid worker in his or her company is making.

What these people are not paying attention to is the difference in skills and responsibility. A few sentences from a mouth of a CEO of a big multinational company can result in billions of dollars of profit. What's the value of those few sentences? How do you measure it?

Compare this responsibility with the responsibility of someone who cleans the floors. There's nothing in what they do that could have the same effect on the company. There's nothing that could even be compared to the scenario above.

Yet even today there are people who believe that there should be some artificial multiple that regulates the difference between the salaries of a toilet cleaner and a CEO of the company.

For example, if a janitor makes $10/hour, they claim that the should be a multiple, say, 18 times, and no one in the company should ever make more than $180/hour.

This conversation is nothing new. It has been going on since the industrial revolution. People were saying the same things about Andrew Carnegie and Henry Ford that they are saying today about Bill Gates and Mark Zuckerberg.

These people have the same formula in their heads when it comes to online coaching. One of the important things to understand is that there's no logic to it.

A lawyer charges X per hour, so a coach shouldn't be charging more than Y per hour.

Your monetary compensation as a coach should be based on a combination of actual value as defined not by you, but by your clients, and by what you can get.

These are the only two criteria that matter and that you should be paying your attention to.

HOW TO THINK TO MAKE MAXIMUM MONEY AS AN ONLINE COACH

Most of the success in being an online coach has to do with what is going on in your head more than anything else. It has to do with your attitude towards money. It has to do with your attitude toward yourself. These are really related to your self-image.

Attitude #1: As a coach, your role should not be of service to clients. Being of service is what servants do, not coaches. Your role is to control clients and to attempt to get compliance from clients.

Attitude #2: Nothing is more important to a successful online coach than a feeling of superiority compared to everyone around you. That's doesn't mean that you have to dislike your clients. This means that you have to be fully aware of how ignorant and dysfunctional most of your clients are.

If you get several clients, most of them will not follow your instructions no matter what you do. You will start thinking that you need better clients. This is no true.

The entire universe continually reorders itself according to the 80/20 or Pareto's principle.

Vilfredo Pareto was an Italian economist who lives in the late XIX and early XX century. When doing a study, he discovered that 80% of the land in Italy belonged to 20% of Italian families. He also notices that 20% of the peapods in his garden contained 80% of the peas.

General Pareto's principle says that in life 20% of the causes are responsible for 80% of the effects.

Here's how this principle works in your everyday life: you wear 20% of your clothes 80% of the time. You spend 80% of your time in 20% of your apartment or home.

This principle will also be at work when you become a coach. 20% of your clients will be getting 80% of the results. No matter what you do with your clients, how you structure your programs and how much you charge, this number will remain the same. You could put twenty billionaires in a coaching program and you still will get the same results: there will be one or two who will be superstars, two to four who would be doing great and then there would be the slow majority.

The best way to develop superiority is to observe people around you and notice how ignorant everybody around you is.

Attitude #3: The attitude that you need to have about money can be explained in the words of Stuart Wilde, a British writer: "When they show up, bill them."

You should never be working for free. There is nothing more futile in life than giving out free advice.

If they don't give you money every step of the way, you will lose your control over them. You will not get compliance from them and you will eventually lose their respect. The respect your clients have for you is in direct correlation to the fact that they have to give you money for everything you do for them.

It is important to understand that in the online coaching business you are not dealing with your own values, but your clients' values. We have already touched on this subject a little when we were discussing about how you should be charging for you clients. We established that you want to move away from charging per hour and move to charging based on the value that you bring to your clients.

The value is about the results to the client. It is not about the results that make sense to you or the results that you'd like to see in your life.

It is also about the relationship with your clients and the clients' perceptions of their results, not your perceptions of their results.

This is very important: The value of your online coaching is all up to them to define and decide about. It's not up to you.

Your attitudes about value need to be about first and foremost making your clients happy and having them want to continue their relationship with you. This is very different from providing the core value, from the nuts and bolts of your specialty and your field.

Attitude #4: This attitude is the willingness to exercise power and control over people and be comfortable while doing so.

As we have already mentioned discussing other attitudes, your online coaching business is about controlling your clients. The big mistake is showing them how much you know, giving them a lot of information and resources, sometimes even for free, and then hoping that they would recognize the value and buy from you.

Unfortunately, this doesn't work. Now, it should work from the logical standpoint, but it doesn't.

This is similar to business people thinking that they should have a line of customers just because they have a great product or service. They think that having a great product or service entitles them to success.

That's not how things work in business. People have no idea how good a product or service is until they actually try it. Getting them to try it is the job of sales and marketing.

This is why you will often see people who do provide great service and who are broke. They are broke because their marketing is bad.

At the same time there are people and businesses whose products or services aren't that great, but who are always doing well. The reason for it is simple: they know how to sell. The best chiropractors don't make the most money among chiropractors, because their incomes have nothing to do with being best chiropractors. Their incomes have everything to do with being known for being the best chiropractor. It's all about what the market believes about you.

A great example of a business that is doing well, but hardly provides the best deliverable is McDonald's. When you go to a McDonald's restaurant, you'll see that it's almost always busy, even though hardly anyone would ever say that a McDonald's burger is the best burger they ever had in their lives.

The reason why McDonald's is busy is simple: McDonald's understands what business they are in. They are in the business of fast food.

The #1 word here is fast: McDonald's has a system that allows them to prepare and deliver the food quickly, much faster than Burger King, for example.

All these other places, such as Burger King, don't understand the business they are in. They think that they are in the food business. They try to compete based on having better food and every time they do, they fail miserably.

Similarly to this, coaches that fail do not understand what the coaching business is about. They think that it's about providing information and a coach that provides the best information and extends himself or herself more to provide services to a client, wins.

In reality coaching is all about exercising control and providing value not based on your ideas and perceptions, but on clients' definition of value. If you deliver a lot of core value, but there is no relationship value, your clients will be leaving you in droves.

This also means that you will be paid for not for what you think you are being paid for. It is also not what your clients think that they are paying for.

Far more than the results you are able to deliver, the quality of your service or the deliverables, you will be getting paid for your reputation.

HOW TO BUILD REPUTATION AS A STARTING ONLINE COACH

One of the easiest ways to build a reputation is to write a book. When you write a book, people around you, your prospects and your friends, automatically give you credit for being smart, for knowing a lot about your field and for being an expert.

Today you can even self-publish a book. You can go to a website like www.Lulu.com, you can upload a PDF file, use a book cover building tool and have your PDF file become a book in a matter of days.

You do not need a book agent, a deal with a publishing house of any of that. You can write a book on your computer and self-publish it. Your self-published book will look like any other book. Most people have no idea what the difference is between a self-published book and a book that's been published through a big publishing house. Not only don't they know the difference, they don't really care and for the purposes of expert positioning as an online coach your self-published book will work just fine.

The next thing that builds your reputation is stories that are being told to your prospects about others. It is very beneficial to a business if you operate in a small niche and can have people tell each other stories about you. These stories with govern your reputation. Nobody questions stories. Nobody investigates stories. People accept them as true when they hear them.

As a side example, the corollary of this lesson is in hiring. One of the first things you should do when hiring anyone is check references. Everybody knows that. However, the national statistics show that only 4% of employers check references of their prospective employees. 96% never bother to make a phone call. These 96% assume that if a person listed a phone number on their resume, then a call would always result is someone saying good things about the person.

It is also important what your prospects and clients read about you. This is why you want to have articles about you on the Internet.

When Tom Peters wrote the book "In Search of Excellence," he described thirty companies in his book that were striving to be excellent. The book made such a buzz that for a short period of time being written about in the book even drove the stock price up. Everybody wanted to do business with companies in the book. People wanted to do joint ventures, buy the companies, merge with the companies, and be acquired by those companies and so on.

The logic was the following: the book talks about excellent companies and a company is in the book, therefore it must be excellent.

That's the power of the written word.

The book "In Search of Excellence" was published back in 1982. There's a reason why we chose such an old book. We can now look at the companies mentioned in this book and see what happened to them in the long run.

Turns out, the commonality that the excellent companies from Tom Peters' book have in common is that they all went bankrupt. They may have been excellent for some period of time, but they all ended up belly up. Arguably, they might have been too busy with being excellent and neglected the issue of being profitable.

The next factor that is of crucial importance to your reputation is who you associate yourself with in their minds. This is especially important if you are just getting started and have no reputation whatsoever.

One of the things to understand about reputation is that you can borrow it and that for marketing purposes borrowed reputation is as good as an owned reputation.

Kevin Federline was able to make significant amounts of money only because he was seen and briefly married to Britney Spears. This is it. No talent, no intellect, no abilities, no skills, no education.

In the summer of 2016 Scott Disick was getting paid up to $50,000 to appear in the nightclubs in the Hamptons on Long Island, New York. What did Disick do? Why is he famous? He appeared on the reality TV show with the Kardashians. This is it. He is famous because he is famous.

Who you are associated with, who you are seen with, who writes a blurb for your book or a guest article for your website, who you interview for your website, who you spend time with, who you reference in your free articles and training materials – all of this matters and adds to your reputation.

The online coaching business is all about creating a reputation and then becoming known for it.

The first thing you need to get started is decide what reputation you want to have. Do you want to be an old wise grumpy veteran of the industry? Do you want to be an arrogant young punk that all the old veterans are annoyed with? Do you want to be nice and warm? Do you want to be obnoxious? What do you want to be?

When you are creating a reputation from scratch, you get to decide all these things. Obviously, you can't be all the things that you currently aren't, so you need to pick features and characteristics that you will be comfortable working with.

In online coaching you are known for your competencies. You are known as a certain type of person. If you want to be effective, you first want to decide what these competencies are going to be.

You may want to be known as somebody who is very difficult to work with. You may want to be known as a very compassionate person. You may want to be known for a certain skill or competency.

You need to make a decision about all these things and create a shortlist. Then the goal is to make sure that you use that list to strategically reinforce it.

You choose a persona and then you build it. It is important to understand that if you don't consciously choose it, you will end up with a reputation anyway. People will still be talking about you, associating you with others and assign competencies to you.

The only difference is that in the approach that we described you get to be in charge and in control. In all other instances you are leaving these matters to chance and your marketplace to figure out.

Another important thing to understand about a reputation is that it's very hard to change once it sets in. This is why you want to give a lot of thought to what you want your shortlist of qualities to be.

There's a way to use strategically everything that you put into your reputation. There's also a matter of condemnation and pardon. Two people can perform the same act, but the public's perception of this act and the attitude towards it will be completely different.

The personal growth coaches have the worst position in terms of this because they teach people about good behavior. Engaging in bad behavior for them is similar to completely burning their reputation.

With this in mind it is important not to commit yourself to a persona that is so incompatible with the real you that you know that at a certain point it will get out and you will get caught.

It is also crucial that you don't commit to things that are not sustainable in the long run as a part of your business.

Let's take a look at this one: "He is an online coach that always emails his clients back within 30 minutes."

This may serve you well early in your online coaching business and may attract some new clients to you.

However, can you sustain this reputation over a long period of time?

If you were to become successful, this is absolutely unsustainable. You may be able to email people back quickly when you have 5-10-20 or them, but if you have 100 or 200 or 1000 and you have to email them back within 30 minutes, you won't be able to physically do it even if you wanted to or even if you stopped eating, showering and sleeping and were answering emails every minute you were awake.

Let's take a look what would happen if you were to use this promise, become successful and then had to break it? All your clients would feel cheated and would get aggravated with you.

This is why you can never set impossible standards. You should develop ones that are sustainable and that facilitate control and power.

Here's another example. If you do group coaching via webinars or online video, a reputation of being compassionate, relaxed and fuzzy is not going to be helpful to you. Sooner or later one of your group coaching participants will break the rules. You will have to discipline them, which is very hard when you are known as a kind and compassionate person. A reputation of someone who can occasionally get really mad for no obvious reasons is actually much more helpful in this scenario.

When thinking about the reputation you want to have, think about your market. What kind of person do your prospects admire? Who do they want to be around? Who do they wish they were? Preferably, you want to choose a persona that has an evergreen appeal, not something that is going to work and be popular today and gone tomorrow.

Also you want to stick with things that are easy for people to understand and remember.

All businesses and business people tend to overestimate their importance in people's lives. Your clients will have tons of responsibilities, commitments and things on their minds. You will be present only in a small part of their lives.

While it is smart to be extending your presence, it is also smart to acknowledge how busy and occupied people are. You want to present your material in small chunks of information. You want your concepts to be simple, so that people could grasp them and remember them even when they are really busy and have a ton of other things going on in their minds.

A great strategy is to develop a short elevator pitch about yourself and what you do. You want your prospect and clients to be able to explain who you are and what you do very quickly and easily.

You need to think very carefully about all of this. This is a really important piece in your future online coaching business puzzle.

People will be asking you questions and expecting certain things from you. Your answers and your behavior will need to be in line with your reputation.

If, for example, you mention a number of books that have nothing to do with the image you are trying to convey, the people will be upset and confused. Your shortlist of things has to become a permanent reference feature that is constantly used and governs all the decisions that you make about your online coaching business.

Being with being known for something you choose, one competency, one characteristic, one story. Then, expand.

WHAT WILL YOU BE KNOWN FOR AS AN ONLINE COACH?

In coaching it is crucial that the heavy lifting, the selling of your services, is done before you actually talk to someone, before they come to you, before you come to them.

This lifting can be done by having articles on your website and on other websites, by having a YouTube channel where you post videos, by conducting interviews and sharing them on your website, iTunes and Soundcloud, by having a funnel, sending out emails and more.

The idea here is simple: you want your reputation to do the work for you beforehand. You may have a big folder of audio and video files that they need to watch and listen. Whatever it is, your prospects need to do some work before they can actually talk to you and you need to strategically craft pieces of information that drive your prospects to you and create an impression of you that you want to create.

You may have a fear that by doing this, that by having a process that your prospects need to go through, you will lose some prospects. The issue here is that without a process your prospects will be completely unprepared. You also will not know what to talk to them about or how to choose them. There is nothing worse in the online coaching business than a communication with a person who doesn't know who you are. This is why it is better to move to the next prospect than to deal with someone who did not go through the process, doesn't know anything about you and is completely unprepared to talk to you.

Here is an example of how some great online coaches sell their services.

A prospect learns about a coach by reading some articles on the internet, watching some videos, reading some testimonials.

The prospect then fills out an online form. They next get an email that asks them about what they are looking for and what results they expect to get from working with the coach. Usually they are asked to write a statement no shorter than one page, but no longer than two pages.

Here's why this is important: this whole process is strange to people. They came to buy something and they are being told that they need to do some work in order to do so. From the very beginning, even before the monetary transaction, the coach is changing the way they normally do business, behave and get things done.

People are used to when they want to buy something and the person selling that something learns about it, that person jumps all over them and tries to close the deal. You do not want to be that person. You want to do the opposite.

You want to make it hard to become your client. You want your prospects to fight to get the opportunity to give you money.

Next, prior to a skype appointment with the coach, a big FedEx package arrives at the prospect's door. The package has books and articles and CDs and DVDs and newsletters and testimonials and more. The package also contains instructions about what to pay attention to first, what to pay attention to second and what to do before they get on skype with their coach.

The reason for sending this package is that the best coaches do not want to be convincing anyone to hire them. They want the prospect convincing the coach about why the prospect is a great fit for the program. The big package is the salesperson that is doing all the selling so that the coach doesn't have to do any of it.

There are two kinds of conversations you want to have with your prospects. The first one is them convincing you why they would be a great client for you. The second is a discussion about when, where and how much. This is it. You do not want to have any other conversations with your prospects.

By the time they actually get to speak to you they will be a little frustrated. They will be a bit anxious, but at the same time by doing all the work to get to that step they have decided to hire you and that's exactly where you want them to be. You want them to emotionally commit to hiring you before they even talk to you.

This may seem like a hard process to build, but in reality it's not harder than to have to sell yourself every single time to people who know nothing about you.

Here's also what's really important about this process: if you get a sale by selling hard, then controlling your clients after the sale will be impossible. They will feel like they are in charge and they can tell you how things are going to be, even though for them to achieve any kind of results it should be the other way around: it should be you telling them what to do and them doing it.

The process also isn't just about a sale. This is about the start of your relationship and the way this relationship will develop.

How it starts determines how it will be developing and how it will end.

The worst thing you can do when selling online coaching is be an impatient salesperson that will do anything and everything to close the deal.

If you are a great salesperson and know how to close deals, not jumping in to close a deal may be hard for you. Your instinctive reaction when somebody wants to give you money may be to get that money in five minutes. However, you can't do that in online coaching. This transaction is only a beginning of a relationship and getting money this way doesn't mean that the relationship is going to develop the way you want it to after you get the money.

This is why you need a process that you can implement whenever you are dealing with a prospective client. Too many coaches care about making the first sale in any way they can and do not put any thought as to what will happen after the sale.

With coaching you can sell clients with brute force. It can be done. However, you can't keep a client for 10 years if that is how you obtained them.

WHAT YOU SELL AS AN ONLINE COACH IS NOT WHAT PEOPLE BUY

In the previous sections of the book we touched on the subject that online coaching is all about exercising control over your clients and delivering value to them in the way they see it, but not in the way you see it.

In this section we will discuss what you are really selling as a coach. What you really sell is not what people think you sell.

First of all, you are not selling credentials. We have discussed earlier the fact that credentials don't matter. We live in a celebrity-driven society and the amount of money you will make is all about what you are known for, whom you are known to and people that you are associated with.

Most of your clients don't know what all the academic credentials mean anyway. The only people that know what all the credentials mean are the people that are issuing the credentials. Also, nobody ever checks the credentials today. Nobody makes any decisions based on formal credentials.

If your prospects are not making their decisions based on credentials, then what is it? You are now probably thinking that it's all about the results that they are going to get in their businesses, relationships or their life.

Success in online coaching is not about delivering tangible results, either.

What your prospects are really buying is your confidence, your certainty, your expertise and the control you will exercise over them from the very beginning of your relationship.

When you sell, it should feel more like a prescription from a doctor: here's what you need, here's the cost, here's how you can pay, here's what happens next. There should be no questions coming from your prospects at this point.

Questions would mean that the process that you have in place is flawed and needs to be fixed. The worst thing that can happen at this stage is your clients telling you: "Well, what if you take this out? Can I replace X with Y? Can I do Z instead of T?" This is not what should be happening.

You prescribe. Here's the fee and they say yes. This has everything to do with confidence, certainty, control, and it has almost nothing to do with anything else, especially all the things that people think you are selling as a coach.

Here's an example. Let's say you needed brain surgery. Which surgeon do you want? The one that will tell you: "Well, you know, the chances of success are hard to predict. I don't claim to be the best in the country in what I do, I mean, I am good, but I am not sure if I am the best. But I will do my best to get you the best outcome I can."

Or do you want the person that will say: "You came to the right place. You are in the right hands now. Relax. We are going to take care of everything, complications are impossible and you'll be ready to go tomorrow."

Logically, most people will say that they want the person that will tell them the truth. However, that's not what happens in reality. People prefer confidence and control to the truth.

How online coaches create self-sabotage

#1: Excessive concern over credentials or educational background.

Nobody cares except for you and nobody will ask you. As long as you look like you went to school and have some kind of a degree, people will assume that you have a degree and won't even bother asking you or checking it.

#2: Concerns about the difference between what you are making and what your clients are making. Not understanding what value provides.

Some people are afraid of becoming online coaches because they will be required to give advice and talk to the people that make way more money than they do.

Your friends and relatives may ask it in the following way: "How dare you coach people who are more successful than you are?"

The answer to this question is that the value that you will deliver to your clients has no relationship and is not governed by the ratio of financial success between your clients and you.

The thing that most people think about when asking this question is a specialized knowledge. They don't realize that there are numerous examples of really affluent people paying much less than they are making for specialized knowledge.

For example, a CEO of a huge multinational company makes more money than any dentist. Yet it doesn't prevent the CEO from going to the dentist on the grounds of making more money. The dentist has skills and knowledge that the CEO doesn't have. That's all that matters.

It is the same in coaching. The fact that someone is making more money than you is absolutely irrelevant.

#3: Experience is not required. Most of deliverables as an online coach have nothing to do with core expertise or experience. They do revolve around asking questions and having common sense.

For years Rory Fatt was one of the most well-known coaches in the restaurant industry. Rory Fatt never owned a restaurant, worked in a restaurant or managed a restaurant. His career prior to becoming a coach for restaurants was working as a salesman for a food service broker and calling on restaurants.

Bill and Steve Harrison are publicity experts that teach people how to get into New York Times, Forbes, The Wall Street Journal and other well-known publications. They have a thriving business and no one has ever asked why they are not famous themselves.

These are just a few examples from the abundant evidence that shows that experience is not necessary.

Here are the real valuables that you bring to the table that are relevant and that do matter. The first one is fresh eyes.

Let's say you coach restaurant owners about their businesses. The owner that has become your client is in his restaurant all the time. He is not seeing all kinds of things that are happening in the restaurant simply because he is too close to them and he is used to them.

As a coach you can walk in and you will see them right away. "Walk in" here doesn't mean walking in physically. You can get the same results with online coaching by talking to someone on skype and asking questions. You could also examine someone's advertising. You do not need to go to the place of business. All you have to do is look at the files that your clients will send you. It could be their brochure. It could be their financial statement. It could be a book of their employee policies. Whatever area you work in, you do have fresh eyes and your clients don't, no matter how much more money compared to you they are making. And that's what really matters in this business.

No matter how successful your clients are, not matter how intelligent they are, no matter how much they know about their business, they do become blind even though they can see.

You can walk in, look around and start asking questions. Why are you doing things this way? Why aren't you doing this this way? Sometimes the questions may look extremely dumb, but there's a huge value in having to answer dumb questions, because they will force people to think about what they are doing and why.

Earl Nightingale, a great American success coach and motivational speaker, said once: "Lock yourself in a room for an hour every morning with no resources, no nothing, and just think about how you could be of greater value in service and interest to your customers."

Now, everyone would agree that this is an absolutely great idea. At the same time, how many people do you think are going to implement it? Nobody is doing it by themselves. They need someone to lock them in a room, give them a pad and a pen and tell them that they can't come out of the room until they write down ten ideas about how they could be of great value and service to their customers. This is the only way to make this work.

This is coaching value that requires no experience whatsoever. All it requires is a key, a pen and a pad. At the same time, this value can be enormous.

If you are a business coach, you want to make your clients defend their ideas. There's enormous value in it, too. The more successful a person is the less people he has around him to challenge him. Pretty soon such a person has a whole bunch of people sitting around a table and agreeing with everything this person is saying; no matter how idiotic, dumb and useless the ideas are.

Simply making such a person defend his ideas has great value to them, because they don't have anybody else to do it. It is okay if they win the argument and the idea turns out to be great or if they refuse to defend an idea. You made them think about it, you did something no one else was going to do and that's what was so valuable about it.

Very often you will have a coaching session, your client will be telling you something and some of their ideas and opportunities are going to leap at you. In most cases your clients will be completely blind and will not see the opportunity before you present it to them. In their businesses people usually have something that they are not paying attention to that is where all the money is.

For a lot of people the value of having an online coach is in being able to tell the people around them that they are doing something because their coach told them to. If it were their idea, it would never happen. Now that the idea belongs to someone else, it will get implemented. There is a lot of value in this, too.

Another big value that you can provide, especially to successful people, is recognition. The more successful a person is, the more likely it is that nobody gives them any recognition. People expect successful people to perform well and be smart. Therefore, when they are, it's not something worthy of praise. It's something normal. You giving them praise has a lot of value in it.

Do you need to offer a guarantee with your coaching?

Here is a very interesting thing about a guarantee: the higher the level of the clients and the higher the price of a product or service that is being sold to them, the less important are the guarantees.

It is the exact opposite of what it seems.

A person buying a $300 item for whom $300 is a lot of money wants to be sure that the item comes with a guarantee.

A person that is buying a $3,000 item doesn't care about a guarantee that much.

A person that is buying a $30,000 item doesn't really care about a guarantee in most cases. It doesn't even matter if $30,000 is a lot of money or not to this person. Now, this many not be true when it comes to commodities like cars, but this is true when it comes to coaching and intangible purchases. To make a $30,000 purchase the person had to get past the point where they need a guarantee reassurance.

HOW TO EXERCISE CONTROL OVER CLIENTS

In the previous sections of the book we mentioned that exercising control over clients is an important part of being an online coach.

In this section we will discuss how you can exercise control and what you need to know and do in order to be able to do so.

The first thing that you need to understand is that you can't abruptly and randomly exercise control. You can't have no bed time for your kids for months and then suddenly decide that there will be a bed time because Uncle Jack will be visiting. Lots of luck with that.

You either have control or you don't have control. We can't not have control and get it occasionally, when you really need it or want it. It doesn't work this way. The only way it works is when you build in control continuously from the beginning and all the way through a relationship.

When you sell your online coaching services in the way we have discussed previously, when you have a process that your prospects need to go through, you begin exercising control with the process. This is something that you can build on later and your further control will not look out of place.

One of the ways to exercise control is to have rules. All the clients need to know the rules. Also, you can't tell them about the rules in the beginning and then just forget about them. Your clients have a lot of things on their minds and remembering your rules is not one of those things. It is really low on their list of priorities.

Also, the more successful your clients are, the less likely they are to follow the rules, because one of the reasons they became successful in the first place is that they are used to breaking the rules.

Your rules need to be simple and clear. You need to remind your clients about the rules a lot.

If you don't have clear rules in your online coaching business and you don't remind your clients about the rules, your coaching environment will be disintegrating to the point where you realize that it's chaos. Putting the chaos genie back in the bottle is not easy.

This especially applies if you do group coaching via webinars and video. If you do have such groups, you want to email a copy of the rules before every meeting. During your group webinar meetings your role as a coach is mostly to play traffic cop and make sure that everything is in order. It is about keeping a few people from dominating the conversation and encouraging shy members of the group to join in.

You will also need to watch the clock, so you can't have three people who talk last have ten minutes a piece when everybody else had an hour a piece. You also can't have people cheating and have someone leave early, right after they got feedback from the group about their situation or their problem. This cannot be happening.

In a one-on-one client relationship you have three the biggest blocks of exercising control.

The first one is that meetings happen when and where it's convenient to you, not to them.

The second one is that there is strict control of their access and they can't reach out to you whenever they want to.

The third one is that you have rules about how your coaching works.

If you don't give your clients any instructions or rules, you can't be upset with them if you are not exercising control.

Another very important part of online coaching is that you want to make people dependent on you.

Werner Earhart is an author, thinker and creator of transformational models and applications. He wrote about leadership, performance, integrity and other subjects. He has lectured at Harvard, University of Chicago, Massachusetts Institute of Technology and Oxford.

Earhart also created Earhart Seminars Training or EST. The organization offered a two-weekend sixty hour course known as "The EST Standard Training." When later asked about EST, Werner said: "We preach independence and we breed dependence."

To a great degree all coaching businesses are the same. You want to be teaching people how to be independent, but at the same time you want them to depend on your training, because they will leave your program if they don't depend on you.

Here's something really important to understand about online coaching. With just about anything you can coach people on; they will get all the mechanics in about a year of being in your online coaching program.

The mechanics of anything aren't really hard or complicated. Therefore, your clients will not depend on you for your core competency for that long. This means that if you want to keep them in your programs for a long time, they need to be dependent on you for other reasons.

Reason #1: It is helpful if they believe that you truly are the only person that can help them. It is not hard to have people believe it. People actually want to believe it. They found you. They like how and what you teach them. They want to believe that you are unique. It is important to them.

Reason #2: It is helpful is there is something mystical about what you do.

For example, Harvey Dent is an American writer of financial newsletters. One of his books, The Great Depression Ahead, appeared on the New York Times Bestseller list in 2009.

Harvey has proprietary software that he talks about all the time. The software helps him calculate trends.

In a similar way you could have a proprietary process for finding overlooked opportunities, your strategies and so on.

It is a mistake to be visible all the time doing everything you are doing. A lot of what you will be doing as an online coach is not that impressive. You do not want people to see the stuff that's not impressive. You want people to be really impressed with you and with what you do.

You can't let them see everything. The best solution to this is to have a "secret cave" where you go to think about their problems and issues and from which you come back with the solutions. Your clients should not be allowed in the "secret cave." Something happens behinds the rocks that they are non-members of. You come out of the cave, bring a solution, they wonder what is happening there, but they can never see it.

You can't let them enter the secret cave because in the absolute majority of the secret caves that are presented as secret caves there is absolutely nothing to see.

There needs to be something magical about what you do in you online programs. This is the second reason that clients will stay with you for a long time

Reason #3: there always needs to be something else, something that will come next.

One of the ways to breed dependence is to have the next thing coming. Now they can't leave because they want to see what's next. You are going to come up with something during your next coaching session that they've never seen before, something that's interesting and exciting and never happened again.

Next year something is going to be different. Every year you want to change your online coaching programs. It may be a very little change, but you do want to change them. If you don't, everyone will be thinking that they've been there, done that, have seen what you have.

Weight Watchers is a great example of how a company that offers training and coaching can be coming up with something new all the time.

Weight Watchers International is an American company that offers various products and services to assist its clients with weight loss and maintenance. It was founded in 1963 in Queens, New York. Today it operates in over 30 countries all around the world.

Weight Watchers has been using points to measure how much food their members can eat. For example, a slice of pizza could be 1 point and so on.

First, every year they slightly change the rules about the points.

Prior to the points they had a new thing every year.

There was a year with a free day deal. One day a week members could eat whatever they wanted and it didn't count.

Next, there was a pick a bad food year. A member could pick some bad food they loved and the bad food didn't count.

As you probably understand, the names of the programs were different and sounded much better. Here we are just giving you examples of how new can be implemented.

MISTAKES TO AVOID IN CLIENT RELATIONSHIPS

The biggest mistake online coaches make in their businesses has to do with becoming too familiar to their clients.

Familiarity breeds contempt.

Friends do not pay friends for coaching. Friends help each other for free. You don't gain power through friendship, you lose it.

The only people that you have even less power over compared to your friends are your family.

Your clients can't call you the way your friends or family can. You need to restrict access. There also needs to be something magical about what you do.

The second they think they've got it all from you, the second they think they know everything you know, they are gone. They will lose interest in you so fast that your head will spin.

This is why you need to be very careful about what you let your clients know, what you let them see and what you don't let them see. If you meet with them in person occasionally, you need to be very careful about how much time you spend with them where they see more and more and more of the real you and less and less of the carefully constructed persona that we discussed earlier in this book.

Next, you want to avoid obligation at all costs. You want people to feel like they are obligated to you. You do not want to have any sorts of obligations to them.

If you do meet with your clients in person in a setting like a restaurant, always pick up the tab. This is a very important behavior because it is symbolic. It says a lot of things about you.

You never want to take an unfair advantage of a client. It is okay for them to do something for you once in a while, but don't have them working for you for free for a week in a row.

Your clients should want to be like you. It may be a mystery to you as to why someone will want to be like you, especially if they make more money than you do. However, they want to be like you because of all the behavior they witness, the confidence, the discipline, the control and the attitude.

They don't want to be like you and they don't want you as their coach if you are crying and you are weak and you complain and moan and your relationships are screwed up, too, and your employees are all idiots and your customers are also stupid. Nobody will want to be like you. People will also feel that you can't give them any good advice, which would mean death to your business.

You can't be sharing things like these with your coaching clients. You can't talk and complain to your clients in ways that undermine their desire to be like you.

Another big mistake that online coaches make is believing that continued participation in your coaching programs, patronage of your business and their interest can be retained as gratitude for past contributions that you've made as a coach. This just doesn't happen.

All coaches hope that this happens, but it never does. The memories of your online coaching clients are remarkably short. They will also be inclined to rewrite history and memories in their minds to reduce the value of your contributions to their accomplishments.

If you want to keep your online coaching clients for a long time, here's what else you should do now: clients will continue their participation in your programs based more on their feelings than the reality. It doesn't matter that reality may include great accomplishments and results on their part.

Online coaching business is a feelings business. It's all about how your clients feel about you, how they feel about themselves and how they feel about the experience that they get while in your coaching program. It's not really about hard results.

Clients will leave you based on their feelings even if they actually have great results. If you are making someone a million dollars, but the person is not having a good time when talking to you, this person will leave you.

You need to carefully assess, control and influence the feelings of your coaching clients. Your business is about how they feel, not about the results.

You need to be able to deliver results, but the difference between okay results and superior results will not lead to superior retention. You don't get retention from results. You get retention from how your clients feel about you.

Next mistake is delivering too much content. Some coaches hope that they will be able to retain clients better if they deliver more content. They add a few more webinars. They do five skype calls instead of three skype calls.

All of these things don't matter, because enough is enough. You may have too little content, but at some point piling up more content is not going to solve your retention issues. On top of this, some people will start dropping out if you give away too much content.

They will feel like they can't go through it all. This means that they feel stupid and nobody likes to feel stupid.

When people have negative feelings, they try to get as far away as possible from whatever is causing the negative feelings. They do not try to correct their behavior, they simply run away. If you are causing negative feelings, they will be running away from you.

HOW TO PRICE YOUR ONLINE COACHING SERVICES

There are two main philosophies about money. The first one is that there is a finite amount of money. This means that if you take someone's money, someone else will have less money.

One of the reasons why corporate clients are sometimes not a good fit for business coaching is because their philosophy of money includes the idea of budgets: they develop a marketing budget for a year in advance.

Here's what's wrong with this picture: it is a predetermined restriction of how much money they can make for entire year because they based it on a formulaic equation.

Your advertising budget should be to spend as much as you can as quickly as you can so that you can turn the money over to sell more, to advertise more and so on.

Another limiting corporate idea is the idea of a market share. Everybody starts with an assumption that there is a pre-determined market size. There are only so many people that are going to do X. There are only so many people that are going to do Y. But what happens if you can make the market bigger? That makes all the bets off.

Similarly to these examples, there are a lot of people who believe that there is a finite amount of money. Each customer has a finite amount that they will spend. They have certain price points that they will not cross. If you become a business coach, your conversations will include discussing statements such as "Our clients will never spend more than $X."

All these predetermined ideas are limiting statements. They have nothing to do with reality.

If you want to see what people will spend money on when they don't have any money, find the worst mobile home park community in your area and drive around it. It will probably be a park with trailers leaning to one side, a couple of crack dealers, kids running with no underwear on and so on.

Now, there will be satellite TVs, there will be dishes mounted on the rooftops of the trailers, there will be stereo systems and computer gaming systems. Truth is, people have money for what they really want or decide to spend their money on. In almost all cases you are underestimating the ability of people to spend money on the things that they want.

If you decide to do business coaching, you will always have clients who will tell you that everyone in their business is a cheapskate or that everybody in their community is poor and everybody buys everything by price only.

Here's how you can deal with this. Ask these clients if there are stores in their community other than Wal-Mart. If everyone in their community only buys things based on price, then there should be no other stores, because no one can beat Wal-Mart on price. So, are there any other stores? Is there a Sears? Macy's? Is there a Target? Next, if you were to drive down the street in a neighborhood where everybody buys on price only, there would be only one brand of a car. It is going to be Kia. There isn't a car that's cheaper than a Kia.

This is why all these objections about prices and money and how money moves mostly have to do with what people believe about money and about price and most people have tons of limiting beliefs about these subjects.

The first thing you need to understand about pricing is that there's a market for every price. There are people who are buying $10 online courses on Udemy. Then there are people who pay $30,000/year and more for coaching from people like Jay Abraham, Dan Kennedy and Dan Sullivan.

It is always useful to remember that transaction size matters a lot. If, for example, you were selling your coaching for $5,000, and then went to $20,000 without any differences in conversion, you have just received $15,000 that you can spend on the experience delivered to the customer and the marketing you do to get the customer.

If you cut this money in half, you can pocket $7,500 and you have $7,500 that you can spend on the experience and on marketing. If you deliver better experience, your reputation will precede you, the word of mouth will work better and you could raise the price again at some point in the future.

A budget of $7,500 would allow you to do almost anything to attract a new client. With such a budget you could get to your goal numbers with much faster speed and less effort.

It is you who decides how much you will charge. There are no formulas. We talked about this in the introduction. You should be getting as much money as you can.

At the same time, you need to remember that the more visible you are, the more successful you are, the more speed you create, the more money you will attract to you.

Simultaneously you will also get a lot of criticism from all kinds of people that are not making as much money as you are. It is important to remember here that the people who are going to be very critical of you wouldn't give you money anyway. No matter what you do, they are not giving you any money. Therefore, from the business perspective these people do not matter.

The biggest factor that attracts money to people is immunity to criticism. Online coaching business is a business of dispensing gold stars to people who want to feel better about themselves. It is very important to not become one of these people.

You are in the business of showing ladders to climb. It is important that you yourself do not start climbing any ladders.

The greatest factor that attracts money is being completely independent of the opinions of others. Why can't you charge more? Because people will criticize me, think that I am greedy, they will stop liking me. It is all about opinions of others. Once you become truly independent, money will start flowing to you like never before.

The only people whose opinions you should care about are the people that are voting with their wallets. Your online coaching business is a business. The main goal of every business is to make money. It is not to please people who are reading about your business somewhere or to please your friends or family. The goal is to make money.

Therefore, the only people whose opinions count are the people that are giving you money. Period. This is the ultimate liberation.

CONCLUSION

Thank you for reading this book. In the beginning of this book we promised to show you how to build a real coaching business, a business that is not a job where you trade hours for dollars.

We started with talking about the differences between a job and a business. A job is something where you get an hourly salary. We discussed what you need to avoid that.

A lot of people think that they need credentials or experience to become a coach. We have examined this subject in great detail.

Next we investigated the issue of money. Can you really be a coach for someone that makes much more money than you do? If so, what do you bring to the table and how does it work?

All successful coaches are known for their reputation. People seek them out and want to do business with them because of the reputation these coaches have. Reputation was in the center of the next chapter in the book.

We have then talked about what you are really selling as an online coach. We covered the issue of exercising control over clients and discussed how you should price your services as an online coach.

We hope you enjoyed the book.

Good luck to you in your new online coaching business!